GOD WILL PROVIDE:

Walking by Faith,
Not by Sight

Len Mac Lellan

 FriesenPress

Suite 300 - 990 Fort St
Victoria, BC, V8V 3K2
Canada

www.friesenpress.com

God Will Provide (From the Bible)
Walk by faith, not by sight (2 Corinthians 5:7)

Pictures for this book were provided by Mary Colleen Photography.

ISBN
978-1-5255-6595-3 (Hardcover)
978-1-5255-6596-0 (Paperback)
978-1-5255-6597-7 (eBook)

1. POETRY, INSPIRATION & RELIGIOUS

Distributed to the trade by The Ingram Book Company

CONTENTS HERIN

GOD WILL PROVIDE

———

These stories, reflections, and poems speak about
both blessedness and human restlessness.
Through it all, I believe God to be
the constant and benevolent provider
of all things good,
as well as serving as our silent consoler
when we find ourselves at a loss.

Life is a joyful, yet arduous journey,
as we stroll or struggle
between its peaks and valleys.
Sometimes we get lost in a fog
and find ourselves alone
with our weakness, doubts, and fear.
As a teacher, husband, and father,
these are the times
when I pray and write the most.
It helps me acknowledge
how I feel at that moment
as I wait patiently
for prayers to be answered.

It is my hope that my words,
crossing these pages like trackways,
will help readers navigate
similar roads a little easier,
knowing that you're really never alone.
God will hear your voice,
and He will place good people along your path
to help get you to where you need to be.

DEDICATION

This book is dedicated to my family,
to God the Provider
who inspires us to be
His hands and feet,
and to St. Rita's Parish
to which the proceeds
of this book will be going
to help pay for
the new gathering centre.

STORYTELLING AND THE ISLAND

BRAVELY SINGING

To an unborn son, quietly singing,
To a boy of one, quietly singing,
To her he runs, quietly singing,
Quietly singing the songs of Cape Breton.

In a grade two class, kindly singing,
The tunes she has, kindly singing,
As clear as glass, kindly singing,
Kindly singing the songs of Cape Breton.

In the month of May, proudly singing,
Gaelic lines we say, proudly singing,
While the piano plays, proudly singing,
Proudly singing the songs of Cape Breton.

Our own roads we took, happily singing,
To learn more of books, happily singing,
And how to cook, happily singing,
Happily singing the songs of Cape Breton.

A degree I take, bravely singing,
Some payments to make, bravely singing,
Ah, for goodness' sake, bravely singing,
Bravely singing the songs of Cape Breton.

The island I leave, sadly singing,
But I shall not grieve, sadly singing,
In God I believe, sadly singing,
Sadly singing the songs of Cape Breton.

One day I'll greet, softly singing,
A dear complete, softly singing,

Each night we'll meet, softly singing,
Softly singing the songs of Cape Breton.

Would you, say I, sweetly singing,
To the one so shy, sweetly singing,
Stay by my side, sweetly singing,
Sweetly singing the songs of Cape Breton.

Now I teach school too, kindly singing,
The old tunes like new, kindly singing,
Like she used to do, kindly singing,
Kindly singing the songs of Cape Breton.

To an unborn son, quietly singing,
She and I as one, quietly singing,
To us he'll run, quietly singing,
Quietly singing the songs of Cape Breton.

GLIMPSES

———

Early morning
on the last day of summer,
our staff rode the school bus north
on the way to Peace River, Alberta.

The sun, not yet visible on the horizon,
lit up the edges
on the low-lying purple clouds
making them appear as if surrounded
by a distant fire blazing.
To my tired eyes,
the effect created in that dark bluish sky
was deeply moving
as sky became water

and feathery clouds transformed
into beautiful islands
bordered by brilliant orange beaches.

I stared out the window for several kilometres
until the sun rose and the light changed,
and with it, the most scenic seascapes
over the prairies.

I thanked God
for the fleeting glimpse of home
never realizing fully until then
how much I missed it.

HEADING HOME

I recall being but three or four years old
and not being able
to keep down food or drink.
Dehydrated and weak,
my parents drove me to the hospital
an hour away
and left me there in the care of the nurses.

The terrifying reality
of being left with masked strangers
far outweighed
any feelings of ill health.
I felt abandoned as I screamed
through the bars of my crib
to be taken home.

I'll never forget the day
I was picked up from the hospital;

the pure elation I felt
crawling into the back seat
beside my sister Darlene.
That moment of reclamation by my family
was emotionally the most powerful memory
I can picture from my early life.

I can only imagine
what it was like for my Papa
who too was taken to the hospital
because of poor health
and was not allowed to return home
once he recovered.

With Nana no longer able to look after him
he was moved into permanent residency
at the seniors' manor
where he patiently waited
to be allowed those brief visits
to the places and faces
he was surely missing.

Getting into the car to go home
for his first weekend visitation
I can only imagine
how Papa must have felt.
Heading down the road towards home,
he must have felt so happy
after being reclaimed at long last,
and perhaps a tad miffed
about why it had taken
his children so long.

STORYTELLER

The tape recorder rolled
as my Papa pondered
back and forth on his rocking chair
mulling over the next narrative
he would thoughtfully unwrap
and gift over to me the listener.

Openly and honestly he spoke
of hard times his family endured
in the nineteen twenties,
when his father Johnny,
blinded, took whatever work
he could lay his hands on
and how his mother Catherine,
soon to be widowed,
took to working and cleaning
outside her home in exchange
for the meat and potatoes
that would keep her eight sons fed.

His survival stories
framed with optimism
resembled bleak windows
lightened with humour
and doors closed
by poverty and tragedy
were pushed aside by
strong faith and resiliency.

I recollect how pleased he was
to have his stories published,
and I was glad to see them enjoyed
by so many who knew him.

LEN MAC LELLAN

Papa only voiced serious reluctance
about sharing them
after a fellow he respected
jested with him saying
he was glad not to have grown up
in a family like his.
I could hear the hurt hidden
in his serious and somber tones.

He never mentioned it again
and soon returned
to his cheerful self
as if he stopped worrying about
what people said concerning a past
that could never be changed,
only accepted.

He focused instead on
the one thing he had control over,
which was his positive attitude
towards his life that was
and his life
that was yet to come.

DONALD JOHNNY MURDOCK'S
HOSPITAL STAY IN 1943

———

There were Italian
prisoners of war there,
English soldiers, wounded.
There was this old fellow,
a civilian, two or three beds down.
He was over seventy or eighty.
He would holler at night.

He was in pain.
The soldiers were saying,
"Shut your so and so mouth!"
No mercy on the old fellow.
I felt sorry for him,
so I went down to talk to him
when I was able to walk a little better.
I went down a couple of times
to talk to the old fellow
and told him who I was
and different things.
So one morning came
and I asked the nurse,
"What happened to him?
Where's he gone?"
"He died last night," she said.
"But he made a will to you."
Three chocolate bars,
a couple packages of Woodbine cigarettes,
and any other little thing
the Red Cross gave him and he didn't use.
He willed them over to me.
Maybe because I was nicer
to him than the rest.
It pays to be nice, I guess.

NANA ALMA AND THE GYPSY

My friend and I went to a fortune teller.
She was a gypsy and had
one of those crystal balls and the cards.
It didn't cost much as long as it was silver.
It didn't matter how small it was,
you just had to cross her hand with the silver.

LEN MAC LELLAN

At the time, I was going with a boy
from Crathorne, England.
That gypsy lady told me
we were going to break up.
She said, "You're going to cross water,
and you're going to take
two children with you."
I didn't even know Don existed then.
Didn't I later cross water
(to Canada in 1946),
and I brought our two children with me.

HOME
(FOR THE MAC NEIL FAMILY)
———

My Aunt Isobel told her young sons
not to worry and promised them
that she would be home
as soon as she was better.

Sick and exhausted from cancer treatments,
she laid silently in her hospital bed
when she felt strong and gentle arms
slide beneath her
and lift her up towards the ceiling
where she could look down upon her body.

Not afraid, but at peace,
a choice she was given
whether to go or to stay
to which she responded
that she wouldn't leave her two boys
without their mom,
and down she softly came

back into her suffering body
that would only grow stronger
from that day forward.

Soon she would return
to the sweet surroundings
of good health and home
and to the welcoming arms
of her husband
and her loving sons
just as she promised.
She dwells there still.

BROTHER

——————

I never had a brother growing up,
but I had my neighbour.
A year older than me,
I loved him like a hero
and I wanted to be like him.
In my eyes, he could throw the farthest,
was the strongest, the smartest,
the funniest, and the nicest guy I knew.
During my childhood, he was the only
true friend I remember having.
Whether it was playing
ball hockey in his basement,
exploring the outdoors,
or hanging out in his room,
I always felt welcome.

In school I remember him always
being there when I needed an ally
or an encouraging word.

LEN MAC LELLAN

After high school I saw him less and less,
but in my heart he was still my friend.
He was the only person who wasn't family
who always remembered
to call me on my birthday.

From time to time I heard about
the drug addiction, the hallucinations,
and the schizophrenia.
Now it's been years since I've seen
or heard from him,
and I often wonder how he is doing.
I received word that he now lives
nearby to Edmonton,
but his brother wasn't allowed
to give out his phone number.

I heard he had changed.

If I could call him
it would bring me joy to hear his voice again
and to reminisce about the childhood we shared,
but a little deeper down I feel almost afraid
of what I would say if he should ask
where my family and I lived
in case he wanted
to come up for a visit.

SPIRIT OF CHRISTMAS

―――――――

While my family and I spend Christmas together
in our warm Western home,
I can't help but think about a tragic moment
that occurred 100 years ago today.

It was then that Mary Ellen Bickerton died
and the people of Port Hood, N.S.
stepped forward and did for her and her family
a great Christian service worthy of remembrance.

It was in November of 1908
when my great-grandmother, Mary Ellen Thompson,
eloped at the tender age of fifteen,
marrying Leonard Bickerton,
a much older man.
In secret they departed from her family
and arrived at Seaside,
the coal-rich area around Port Hood.
Leonard found work as a miner
and Mary Ellen would eventually tend
to the needs of their three young girls.

Unfortunately for them,
a long life together was not meant to be.
Just days before Christmas on December 19th, 1914,
it must have seemed like a hopeless situation
to young Mary Ellen.
Her husband was gone and she
was now lying in bed dying of pneumonia
with her beloved children huddled around her.

In the cold darkness did all appear lost
to this dainty, blue-eyed English immigrant
as her short life drew to a close?
Could she have imagined that God would soon
open a new window
so that the light of love would shine again
on her little family?

For a warm light of kindness and compassion
would shine brightly

from the hearts of true neighbours
as they did what they could for the family
but in the end could not save Mary Ellen.
They saw to her funeral
while taking merciful care of her children
until new loving homes could be found.

It seems like such a sad moment in time
if one dwelled on it,
although from one family's ashes
sprung beautiful examples of Christian charity
as the lives of my grandmother and her sisters
were soon begun anew
with three welcoming Port Hood families
in the true spirit of Christmas.

PRAIRIE STORY FROM THE 1930S
(FOR RITA SMITH)

———

Watching through frosty window panes
for her husband's return she hoped.
Mary's mind played deceptive games
as it struggled to grasp and cope.

With her man now dead and buried,
she foresaw slim chances ahead
for the newborn babe she carried
and the seven huddled in bed.

In the cellar stowed winter food
was consumed by ravenous frost,

promising only lean days due
with all hope of survival lost.

For her kids to sleep she waited
in the lantern's despairing light.
To spare them the hunger fated
she'd extinguish their lives that night.

From the darkness reached out a voice
revealing all would be okay,
if she but make the wiser choice
of awaiting the break of day.

Sleep, sweet sleep before her waking
when she heard the knocks at her door,
found morning and neighbours waiting
with wagons, provisions, and more.

Once bound to grief and certain death
now mercifully unfettered.
Saved by the kindness of neighbours
their lives blossomed for the better.

She believed God's voice spoke that night
and never again felt alone.
Throughout Mary's life faith shone bright
'til her Saviour beckoned her home.

RIVER OF PEACE

On the land of the Dunne-za
where numerous ancient trails cross
a small family was buried
and all knowledge of them was lost.

LEN MAC LELLAN

Time passed by as the river flowed
and the earth eroded away
and those bones buried long ago
once again saw the light of day.

Tribal spiritual leaders
were told of the human remains
the three exhumed laid side by side
and reburials were arranged.

On the day of re-interment
people lined the humble gravesite
when three eagles came gliding in
and on nearby tree did alight.

The two adults and an eaglet
eyed the ceremony below
as the bones and found belongings
were respectfully placed just so.

Many onlookers got the chills
recalling when the elders said
how animals of the forest
could carry spirits of the dead.

Once Mother Earth was gently laid
and the prayers were solemnly done
the eagle trio took to wing
to rise again towards the sun.

Numerous ancient trails do cross
where the Dunne-za still abide
travelling high on restful paths
above the peaceful river, glide.

CAIRN OF KINDNESS

In my mind a cairn
of kindred stones was made
from selfless acts of kindness
and true sincerity
all done just for me.

These dear deeds attest
to depths of human hearts
whose turns couldn't be counted
only celebrated
and then passed along.

Who were once strangers
are now warmly familiar
since the monument fashioned
was with kind gentle hands
like God intended.

GREAT AUNT BESSIE AND THE GYPSY

My mother, Sarah, had a gypsy lady
come to the door.
She was good to give them things.
The gypsy opened her hand
to tell her fortune
but closed her hand
without saying anything.

My mother was pregnant
and there was talk
of our family moving

to a bigger house.
When she was asked
when they were going to move,
she said that the only place
she was going was a box.
Not long after, in 1936,
she died while having twins.
The boy was buried
in my mother's arms.
They never got the other one out.

BESSIE
———

Yesterday I learned
that my great aunt Bessie
had died at the age of 100.
She passed two years ago.
She was the oldest
of my nana's sisters and
was her last surviving sibling.

In 2002, I got to know you
when I went over to Northern England
for a week-long visit.
Though I was a lone traveller
I never once felt lonely the entire time.
You lavished me with your priceless gifts
of undivided time and warm hospitality.
You nourished me with endearing stories
that will now endure as long as I breathe.
I will always remember our carefree travels
with your son Edward
to places that I had only heard about
and who can forget the pints we shared?

Thank you, Bessie,
for our special time together.
You were so good to me.
Finding your obituary on the Internet
has done nothing to change
my sentimental notion
that you're still waiting across the ocean
for a return visit.
You, as alive and spry as ever,
tending your garden
with two cups of hot tea
standing at the ready.

BEYOND A DOUBT

It always gets my heart speeding,
my chest tightens and my legs shake.
I look over the church seating
and proclaim a decent reading,
for it was for Him, not my sake.

VOICE IN THE DARKNESS
(TO DOROTHY MAC DONALD)

Mary Jane Cameron never again lost heart,
no matter how dark
moments in her life seemed,
knowing that her mother
could always find her.

At a tender age, Mary Jane was taken in,
as were her six siblings,

by neighbours and relatives
after their mother passed
and their father moved away to work.
The Boyd family had children of their own,
yet they made room enough for young Mary
who worked so hard to please them
and did whatever was expected of her.

One evening the cows were still out to pasture
and Mary Jane was sent to bring them home.
She left the house and ventured out alone
not knowing exactly where they might be.
After some distance she could not find them
and she began to cry in the darkness
feeling lost and afraid.

Soon she realized that she was not alone
when she heard the calming voice
of a woman asking what was wrong.
Mary Jane answered
that she had to bring back the cows
but she didn't know where they were.
The lady's voice reassured her
that everything would be okay
and she would find the cows
up in the field farther.
Mary Jane wasted no time
as she quickly made her way in that direction
until sure enough she found them
and turned them for home.

Mary Jane would always think back
to that night with thankfulness
for the help she received
and would never again lose heart,
even in her darkest hours,

knowing that her mother
could always find her.

MY FIRST NIGHT HOME

After a few enjoyable hours of crib tomfoolery
with my sister and parents,
I retired to my old bedroom
where I closed my eyes
and listened sleepily
to the falling of gentle rain
out in the damp darkness
and the soft clatter of the rocky stream
just beyond my open window.

My mind and body eased into restful bliss
as I felt the soothing touch
of a breeze's feathery fingers
move across my shoulders,
smelling of Atlantic sea salt
and sweet wild roses.

I thrust my aching body up from my mattress,
picked up my pen,
and wrote down these simple words
so I would not forget
when I was far from home years from now
searching for memories
and longing to remember.

OPEN WINDOW

The Northumberland Strait is a stretch of water
between the red shores of Prince Edward Island
and my home province of Nova Scotia.

For over an hour, my wife, children, and I
steadily plied our way
through its dark green waves
and seething white foam
one warm August day this past summer.
Many times, as I stood by an open window
on the passenger deck, my thoughts
seemed to slip away into the ferry's wake,
drifting back to an earlier time
when my great-grandmother
and her brother were sent
across these same waters.

In the late 1850s, Thomas Ryan died,
leaving his wife with twelve children,
some rented farmland, and few choices.
As was the custom for the poor in those days,
Mrs. Ryan spread out her youngest children
to be brought up among friends,
neighbours, and relatives.
Her youngest child, three-year-old Elizabeth,
was sent with her brother, ten-year-old John,
by ship from Cardigan River,
Prince Edward Island.
Safely across the choppy Northumberland Strait
the pair landed on Cape Breton Island
and were taken over land
to River Denys Mountain
to live with their uncle John O'Brien

and his family.
There, Elizabeth and John were nurtured in faith
and each eventually married
and had families of their own.

I cannot imagine the heartbreak
Mrs. Thomas Ryan felt
after losing her husband
and having to hug and kiss
her children one last time
before sending them away,
knowing there were no plans for their return.
Maybe it was best for her
not to even think about it.
Such decisions were made for survival's sake.

Likely there were nights when
my great-great-grandmother's mind
was shrouded in sorrow and doubt
about the decisions she made for her children.
If so, and I had the power to do it,
I'd walk back in time and into
one of her restless sleeps
where I would tell her not to worry,
that when doors were closed,
God opened a window,
and that her decisions made
were the right ones.

TINTIN

———

Buried in a pile at Sears, reduced to clear,
lay a single copy of *Tintin: Hergé and His Creations*.
The $2.99 sticker price on the book's brilliant yellow cover

was by no means a fair appraisal in my mind
since its stories and characters
held such a high intrinsic value for me.

Before 1983, the year Tintin walked into my life,
reading was difficult for me.
I wanted to read during those elementary years,
but it was painfully hard
as I wrestled with every sound
and stumbled over any word greater than two syllables.
I hated the sound of my own voice
as I heard it butcher each sentence into meaningless bits.
My feelings of inferiority and reluctance to read
dragged on for years
until Mrs. Downie, who was my grade seven teacher,
and Tintin changed all that.
It was then that I was first drawn in
by the colourful illustrations
and engaging storylines of the Tintin series.
Since I was allowed to take the graphic novels home,
I was enthralled night after night by each new adventure.
They were the first books
that I remember wanting to finish.
I loved Tintin and his friends so much
that later in life, when I could afford to,
I bought the entire series.
I still keep them boxed up and tucked away
securely in my safe
for the sole intention that maybe
my own son or daughters might need Tintin,
and he would come running
through the densest jungle
or across the most arid desert to the rescue
just as he had done
for me.

THAT'S WHAT FAMILY IS FOR

As a boy with my parents
I only visited my grandmother, Marie,
my Uncle Peter, and my Great-aunt Mary Ann
once or twice a year during the holidays.
I remember it being a house
that I couldn't wait to leave.

The heat from the wood stove in the kitchen
was all engulfing,
drinking water sat unappealingly in an open,
galvanized-steel basin in the corner,
and any thoughts of using the outhouse
caused an immediate, involuntary suppression
of all bodily functions.
It seems silly now
how I stood sweating by the open door
waiting impatiently to make my escape,
wondering why the adult conversation
took so long to finish.

Only years later as a young man
did I finally get to know
these kind and gentle people.
With maturity came service to family
and my contribution
was mowing their grass
in the summertime.
The easy toil was followed
by a customary glass of icy diet 7-Up
from Aunt Irene and a relaxing visit
with Marie and Mary Ann
in their shady living room.
It was there that I began to take a serious interest

in the Gaelic songs and the old stories
that flowed from my great-aunt
like a bubbly mountain spring.
I was genuinely moved as she shared
intimate recollections about my ancestors,
the untimely deaths,
and supernatural encounters
that seemed eerily commonplace.

When it was time to go
the ladies always expressed
such sincere appreciation for the mowing
as my Aunt Irene reached out
to stuff cash into my pocket from a cupboard jar.
I always refused the generous sum
because helping them was something
the whole family did
and I wanted to do it too.
So I would reiterate what I heard my uncle say
whenever the ladies wanted to repay him
for his kindness.
I'd simply repeat
with the fullest of conviction,
"That's what family is for."

GOOD AS GOLD

If you pan Alberta streams
you won't strike it rich I'm told
but you may just walk away
with a tale as good as gold.

In life, he panned gold pockets
along shallow river sides

packed saddle bags with fine gold
on the day before he died.

Seasons came and seasons went
before a prospector came.
He camped on the river's edge
within the panner's domain.

First night he was awakened
feeling colder than he should,
wide-eyed he stared past his feet
to where a bearded ghost stood.

He felt his hair stand on end
as his heart drummed in his chest
but the spectre meant no harm
for he too was seeking rest.

The ghost told of hidden gold
on a saddled branch it sits
'twas there for the taking, since
he wouldn't be back for it.

Next morn away he wended
with the fever on his mind,
hoping that the sun was not
the only thing gold he'd find.

He scanned all the branches low
but found nothing to speak of
until something caught his eye
high in a tree top above.

Knotted on a tree branch sat
a saddle, weathered and brown,

from his gear he drew his axe
in order to bring it down.

He climbed a slow upward path
amid tangled clenching limbs,
soon down it came with a thump
laden branch, followed by him.

He searched the mound of leather
with each pocket took his time,
but all of them were empty
making no reason or rhyme.

So if you pan northern streams,
you won't strike it rich I'm told,
but you may just walk away
with a tale as good as gold.

WAR BRIDE ALMA MACDONALD ON THE *QUEEN MARY IN* 1946

We had to wait to get
our passages from the government,
then you had to move quickly.
We went down to London,
then went to Southampton,
where we left on the *Queen Mary*.
They had nice beds for them,
but John being a baby,
he hung on the side of Elizabeth's bunk.
It was all made of fish netting
so when the boat swayed, it would sway
and he wouldn't get hurt.
Good meals, lots of entertainment,

music, dancing, swimming pool,
and shuffle board.

It was like a little city.
Half were Americans
and half were Canadians.
They were like foreigners
as far as we were concerned;
we were the Canadians
and they were the Americans.
They thought they were better
than we were because
they married Americans.
They thought they were big stuff.

Well, that's how the Americans
thought when they were over in England too.
They thought they were better than anybody else.
Yet they left more babies
and poor girls over there than enough
and wouldn't take them back with them.
No way.

GIVER OF LOVE

———

Before my nana passed
she said she never missed
anything that she gave away.
She was the greatest giver
I have ever known.
A giver of loyalty to the family.
A giver of gifts on Christmas morning.
A giver of warm welcomes
to friends and neighbours.

LEN MAC LELLAN

A giver of hot tea or homemade wine
to the visitor.
A giver of hospitality
to the grandchildren from away.
A giver of scrumptious breakfasts
to the late riser.
A giver of discipline to the bold.
A giver of direction
to the lost or uncertain.
A giver of comfort
to the needy or lonely.
A giver of hope to the disillusioned.
A giver of forgiveness to the offender.
A giver of Christian service
to the stranger and community.
A giver of hugs and unconditional love
to the children.
A giver of fond farewells
as she said,
"Bye for now, sweetheart,"
before I turned and walked away.

NOT ALL THERE

It is a strange feeling entering into a loved one's home
when you know that they are no longer physically there.
So it was on the funeral day after landing "down home"
where our nana and papa lived for so many years.

With much of the day's physical and emotion burdens lifted,
the family members present ate and drank into the evening.
At first the house felt different for its walls seemed like
a shell surrounding a heart that was no longer beating.

Eventually we brought the old place back to life again
for a few precious hours with new stories and laughter.
Near evening's end I imagined that Nana and Papa would
walk through the front door late from bingo or Mass.

How the house would have erupted to jubilant and ecstatic
cries of welcome relief after such an unexpected arrival.
Followed by an eerie silence with the dawning realization
that either they or we, were not all there.

CLOSURE
(FOR MY NANA AND PAPA)

I saw your stars above me fall
like momentary streaks of fire.
And through those celestial wonders
received the closure I desired.

It wasn't found in Cape Breton
in the old house that once was yours.
Nor on pathways you once had walked
above rugged West Mabou shores.

It wasn't seen amid neighbours
or on the faces you had known.
Wasn't heard in conversation
nor on the fiddle tapes you owned.

It was found back in Alberta
after my trip back East was done.
With my heart running on empty
I prayed for some healing to come.

On that long road from the airport
in the darkness above we eyed.
One star fell, and then another,
as they lit trails of light then died.

There one second and gone the next
was a fitting image I thought.
After some silent reflection
I received the closure I sought.

Throughout my life my grandparents
were so giving and inspiring.
They were the North Stars of my sky
whom I looked up to, admiring.

Now I pray for them in that place
where there's peace and goodness galore.
No more pain, together again
with God and family once more.

Not forgotten, cherished fallen
your memory will never fade.
Your descendants will know your names
and the sacrifices you made.

One final wish upon your stars
please continue to be our guides.
We'll journey through with help from you
'til our souls too, alighted fly.

IN RETROSPECT

It wasn't just the shared stories,
homemade wine, pies, and cookies
that made my overnight stays
at my nana and papa's
memorable and precious to me.

What mattered most were the feelings I felt
in those peaceful and unhurried surroundings.
When just being there was enough
to make me feel as if I was the centre
of their kind and caring world.

I'd like to think that a piece of that world
still exists in my own home
where my children and I
now cultivate time together
making new memories
so that they too will know what it feels like
to be truly rooted in love.

ONE KIND OR ANOTHER

In his heart kindness dwelled
as a ready gift to be shared with all
who crossed his path.
He didn't have motives for such giving,
didn't need to know names or circumstances,
nor did he expect anything in return.
Giving was freely done because he knew of the joy
that came from two hearts connected in kindness.

He also knew frustration when his sincerity
was met with suspicion,
was taken advantage of
or was ignored altogether.
Though discouraged by situations
beyond his control
he was never long deterred
after reflection and prayer soon had him
ready again to journey onward.

When he needed kindness
he found himself to be the humble receiver
of unforeseen blessings that would literally
come up to meet him in the most unlikely of places.

Such as the Halifax airport
walking off the airplane into the terminal
when he was touched wholeheartedly
by several random acts of thoughtfulness
from total strangers.

The best way he could describe the experience
was as if he had just returned
from a different world
to find himself back on his home planet
and was once again surrounded
by familiar beings
of the most welcoming kind.

FAMILY AND COMMUNITY

UP WHERE WE BELONG

I found the one for me
only when I knew what to look for.
We shared the same faith,
goals, and values
and the attraction was undeniably strong.

Being from different countries
culturally distinct from each other
scepticism naturally arose
about a lasting union.
We stood at the cusp
of our relationship
like fledglings
uncertain about how well
a lifelong commitment would fly.

Seeing some hesitation in my eyes
Maureen told me
that if I didn't love her
that she would go
if I wanted her to.
It was then that I knew
I never wanted to lose her.

On that very day
unfettered by further doubt
the pair of us took wing
and began our ascension
to the challenging
and rewarding new heights
as one.

HOPE FILLED GOWN

The cutest baby's gown, we bought white and fine
with hopes it would be our baby's in due time.
Years of waiting was a discouraging sign
so we gave it away to a friend of mine.
We told her that we just had to let it go,
a blatant reminder hanging there just so.
This precious gift is just right for you we know,
it will surely make your baby's beauty glow.
We put the gown behind us until one day,
after Alexis was born, what came our way?
A special return gesture to us was made,
at the bottom of a gift bag there it lay.
It was like we remembered, white and fine still,
how much we still loved it wasn't clear until.
It was our gown of hope and forever will,
since it came home to us as a hope fulfilled.

STILL HER DAD

Little sounds in the night
stirred me from restless sleep
as my heart changed its beat
senses raised to new heights.

Listened for further sounds
quieted my own breath
alerted of distress
waited to leap and bound.

Away the sounds had died
to life I awakened

to my feet I'd taken
and soon stood by her side.

Such a scramble I'd done
not many hours before
as I will, later, more
all for this little one.

During those times I had
a hope I attended
my dream hadn't ended
and I was still her Dad.

HAPPY BIRTHDAY
———

My wife quietly eased her way into our room
holding our daughter
just before the 7 a.m. alarm sounded
and commenced singing
a joyful "Happy Birthday",
with smiles beaming wide,
as Alexis clapped her hands.
I knew in that instant that all the cards and cake
that I might receive that day
would seem entirely insignificant
in comparison to what I had just received.
For I truly believed that I had already been given
two of the most precious gifts in the world.

FIRST FAMILY DAY

The highlight of this sparkling wintry day
was pulling our girl on her purple sleigh.
She was bundled up in her brown snowsuit
as she stared at the trees along the route.
Though she made no sounds as I slowly paced,
pure excitement shone on her hooded face.
We were in no hurry to get somewhere,
just leisurely strolled through the fresh cool air.
Before long she was in a peaceful sleep,
a sight I'll treasure and forever keep.
It's taken years for life to get this good,
for so long I just never thought it would.
I ask myself now since I have found love,
what was it that I was so afraid of?

WHITE AND RED

With joyful appreciation
I watch our children frolic
in the newly fallen snow.
They roll around in it
and melt it on their tongues by the mitten full
like colorless cotton candy.
Frosted toques resemble overturned flower pots
as frigid cheeks blossom into plump poppy petals.
The crimson sun completes its restful plunge
into a fiery western horizon,
setting the sky aflame
with a beautiful succession of reds and oranges,
bathing even the eastern moon
in its dying ember light.

Smoky white ribbons from houses nestled nearby
reach silently skyward
like warm prayers of thanksgiving
to those who died for us.
For the happiness
my family and I now enjoy
in peaceful surroundings such as these
under our free fluttering colours
of white and red,
begotten of their very
flesh and blood.

NEWBORN TWINS

This will seem like a blur looking back one day
if chronic sleep deprivation has its way.
There's less time to get done what we used to do
as we focus on the needs to get us through.
Feeding, burping, changing, carefully holding,
rocking, singing, soothing, washing then folding.
Money is scarcer, our movements restricted
from quiet solitude we're now evicted.
Self-pity runs high, energy out of sorts
our eyelids hang low and our patience is short.
Commitment, faith, and love will see us prevail
though I now understand why some have failed.
All would be lost if the good things got outweighed
by urges to lash out, quit, or to run away.

SUMMER OF 2015

Some go to distant places
others work their day away.
My chosen path is different
and I walk it every day.

Keeping up to Alexis
as she peddles down the road.
Training wheels just a rattling
singing her songs as she goes.

With the twins I go strolling
at a nice and easy pace.
They watch with silent wonder
at the beauty of this place.

Most trails and streets seem quiet
with the odd truck rumbling by.
We share time with seniors
who always stop to say hi.

It took a while to accept
that this was my summer's course.
Enjoyment dawned when I saw
this time was a gift, not forced.

Time to spend with my children
a blessing I almost missed.
Who thought finding contentment
would be as easy as this?

TRUEST FORM OF LOVE
(FOR ALEXIS, ALLAN, AND ANNA)

Do we love the ones we covet
when it's selfish and unrefined?
What of crushes and sweet romance
and other constructs of the mind?
Can we make it with our bodies
or conjure it from rhyme or words?
No I say, there's a truer way:
We best love the ones we serve.

LOVE FOR OUR CHILDREN

May they always feel loved
enduring and life long
never ending sweet song
true fondness from above
even after I'm gone.

SUMMER STROLLS

We never missed a day.
Each summer morning
all I had to say was, "Go for a ride?"
and Alexis would make her way
straight to the front door.

We would leave
while the sun was still low on the horizon.
With a bright blue sky above

and the sun at my back
I would see my long shadow
pointing our way forward.

Once the wheels were turning
Alexis never made a peep
secure under her fleece blanket,
looking contentedly in all directions,
soaking in every sight and sound.
I, in peaceful appreciation,
slowly sauntered behind
completely unfazed
by work worries or schedules.

It didn't matter much
that I was the only man
pushing a baby stroller down the street.
I felt proud doing it.
I also knew that each peaceful lull
was a testament to the contentment
Alexis was experiencing.
Sensing her enjoyment
was sufficient motivation
for me to push on day after day.

Soon it was summer's end
and we began to stroll by trees
in the process of shedding
their orange and yellow fall fashions.
Their parched attire crackled under foot
as I thought back to each unforgettable moment
of our second summer together
and I thanked God for it.

Those simple mornings will forever
be imprinted on my mind alone

and I'm sure there will be many more
of such summers to explore and share
but I know no other
will be the same
as sweet.

THOUGHTS IN PASSING

———

All of the poetry and prose that I have ever written
was done in quiet solitude,
away from the distractions of noise and disruption,
as were my most meaningful prayers
spoken in unbroken silence
where true inspiration and God could be found.

BEFORE I FORGET

———

So many precious moments, where to begin?
"Silly Daddy," she says with a laugh and grin.
Playing hide and seek, almost counting to ten.
To and fro on the swing again and again.
Sharing my baloney and watching me shave.
"Again" she blurts after the tickles I gave.
Floating in the pool or in the bath splashing.
Playing horsy games then down the hall dashing.
Sleeping in the backseat, while sucking her thumb.
"Me and you, Daddy?" as she readies for fun.
Watching her run towards me with arms outstretched.
Hugging my leg announcing, "Dad, you're the best!"
How fortunate I am and other such men,
to have time to revisit childhood again.
As the day turns to night to her bed she goes.

LEN MAC LELLAN

She follows our routine to show that she knows.
A story, the Lord's Prayer, and back rub you see.
A kiss and request, "Can you put my blankie?"
As I leave she softly says, "Good night, Daddy."
No sweeter words could be said if you asked me.
But my favourite word of all that she's said,
follows once Maureen and I crawl into bed.
"Together?" we'll hear an inquiring call,
as Alexis watches from across the hall.
"Yes, come," we'll say and she is soon in between.
Joy and excitement on her face can be seen.
For a short time we play and laugh together.
Soon tired old bones seem light as a feather.
What may not seem like much, these simple forays,
yet all were the favourite parts of my day.

A FATHER'S LOVE

———

Take my hand when I'm not there.
Reach my ears in quiet prayer.
Find my peace on moonlight walks.
Seek me out for silent talks.
Find my kiss on morning rays.
Share my warmth on sunlit days.
Feel my hug in wind's embrace.
Scan blue skies and see my face.
Hear my words as wild geese call,
listen close, I love you all.

THE LIGHTEST OF BURDENS

I am like a draft horse pulling twin drivers
in their black plastic carriage.
The nylon tether digs into my waist
as I lean relentlessly forward.
Behind me milestones are marked
by little voices saying, "Bye fountain,"
or "Bye, bye, playground."

My stare seldom reaches the wide grey sky above
as I search for snow cover on the slow trail ahead.
On the black ice my slippery grip does not falter.
The sound of sled on soft snow
awakens my imagination
as I liken it to rustling summer leaves
or perhaps a rocky stream flowing nearby.
Peaceful monotony is only broken
by sudden rough patches
that seem to rip into the sledge bottom.

In the distance I see our welcome stable
where there will be water and a warm place to lie down.
Later they will ride me
across carpet pastures in the basement.
Indeed, I sometimes feel like a beast of burden.
Oh, but what a precious
and beautiful load
I carry.

CHERISH EVERY CHANCE TO...

watch them silently sleep
take them for a relaxing walk
feel wet kisses on your cheek
hear the cute way they talk
see them cuddling together
tuck them softly into bed
play in cool snowy weather
listen to sweet prayers said
enjoy a silly game or dance
feel the cool tub splashes
find them hiding by chance
watch their playful dashes
hear their joyful laughter
watch them eat messy snacks
feel their loving hugs after
give tickles on their back
listen to their happy songs
delight in their bright smiles
teach them right from wrong
hold their hand for a while
dry their warm tears
carry them in your arms
calm their anxious fears
protect them from all harm
hear them call out your name
think they will never change

BREAKFAST RUSH

Rushing through breakfast
I hurriedly glanced up at the clock before school
as the kids finished off their pancakes and bacon
except for my son Allan who hadn't even started
and was trying to push down a freshly cut orange slice
onto the rim of his cup, when suddenly it spilled over
unleashing a torrent of sticky orange juice
across the table.
Though the occurrence wasn't that uncommon
and was in the past of no great consequence
on this particular morning
I slapped my son's hand in anger
which in turn caused his plate to flip over
sending pancakes and syrup
all over his pyjamas and onto the floor.

I held my tongue knowing
I had just compounded a messy situation
and I let him sit there embarrassed
in shocked silence with his head down.
I cleaned up what I had a hand in creating
and then I brought him a new plate of pancakes
and a fresh cup of juice, but he would not eat,
let alone lift his eyes above the top of the table.
Telling him in a cold indifferent tone
that it was an accident
and to start eating his breakfast
did nothing to move his hand towards his fork.
Only after I sat down with my breakfast plate
did I really look over at him
and I could see the shame
and humiliation on his face.
I knew I had hurt him.

LEN MAC LELLAN

I got up and knelt beside him
and whispered sincerely into his ear
that I was sorry for slapping his hand
and that it was my fault
for spilling his breakfast.
I told him I loved him and I kissed him.

Moments later we were eating
our pancakes together
with our appetites and inner peace restored
united in love and forgiveness
and humbly aware
that we were both human
and that we all make mistakes.

THE TRAP

You might have thought we had an infestation
of leprechauns in our living room.
Employing an idea from kindergarten class
my daughter Alexis strung up a pipe-cleaner zip line
that led conspicuously to a leprechaun trap
consisting of a tall upright tin can
cleverly baited with green sunglasses.

Enlisting our support early the next morning
she examined the trap and found it encircled
with tiny footprints
strangely fashioned from lime-green paper.
She was so excited that she had me drag
the couch away from the wall
which uncovered an obscure leprechaun lair,
complete with a collection of Kleenex, lost toys,
and dehydrated fruit.

As our daughter went about searching
for the elf's whereabouts
I smiled thinking back
to my own childhood moments
of wonder and excitement.

As a father I don't look forward to
one day explaining away
any of my children's beautiful illusions
and seeing even the slightest flicker
of betrayal in their eyes.

To the contrary
I want them to believe
that God loves them
and hears their prayers,
and to know that Jesus, Heaven,
guardian angels, and miracles
are all for real.

GOOD-BYES

While in a rush to go out to work
and within proximity of our front door
I reached for my coat when I heard, "Bye, bye!"
from two-year-old Allan
as he and his sister sat watching
from their high chairs eating their pancakes.
I had forgotten to say good-bye
and was almost out the door
before his sweet reminder.
I dropped everything and gave them each a kiss
on their syrupy cheeks
and told them that I loved them.

LEN MAC LELLAN

Walking out to the car I considered
how easy it was to take lightly or to overlook
the importance of parting words
we say to our loved ones.
We assume that all separations are temporary
and there will always be a next time
when we'll see each other again.
With time, illusions fade
as more and more farewells become permanent
and we are left to think about what we didn't say
when we had the chance.
So why wait until it's too late?

So the next time you see me
don't be alarmed if I firmly shake your hand
and look you straight in the eye
as I sincerely thank you for any kindness
that you may have shown me in the past.
And just before we say good-bye
I might be courageous enough
to tell you with all honesty
how I truly feel about you
be it love, or otherwise.

TOGETHER IN FAITH

Years ago we received word
that my mother-in-law tested positive for TB
and required isolation here in our home
with no outside visitors for two weeks
or until further notice.
I was stunned thinking tuberculosis
to be almost extinct,
a plague of the past before modern medicine,

when the so-called "consumption"
swallowed so many lives,
like my grand-uncle Finlay MacDonald
back in the dirty thirties.

Understandably we were shocked,
as was she, crying and pleading
for a plane ticket home to the Philippines,
not wanting to be a burden on all of us.
My thoughts spun as I made my escape
to the walking path
as I prayed to God to steady me
and to provide the right words
by the time I got home.
He did not fail me.
With all the calm I could gather I told her
that staying in Canada was the best option
since the medical community
was on top of it.
I told her that it wasn't her fault
and that nothing in the house needed to change.
I wanted her to know that we weren't angry
and didn't see her as a threat to us.
We as a family were here to support her
and we would get through this together.

During the year-long regimen of penicillin
that was to follow
the risks were eliminated and she was cured.
During that time we never dwelled on
the what nows, the what ifs,
or the dark unknowns.
It was enough for us to just know
and to trust our local medical professionals
and in God.
They did not fail us.

LEN MAC LELLAN

CAREGIVER
(TO THE MUNOZ FAMILY)

———

Though the past three years for me
have seemed to suddenly fly
not so for my sister Fe
who many a night has cried
so quietly in her bed
far from family and home
waiting, working every day,
trying less to feel alone.

Her pay goes across the sea
and some she has called her own
to buy things she's needed most
like the minutes on her phone
so she'll hear her kids again
and her husband's whispers clear
reminding her why she came
of a day when they'll be here.

To be united once more
after living worlds apart
to hug loved ones once again
and feel them so close to heart
as they begin life anew
in Canada's cold weather
but they'll be warm and happy
now that they are together.

JUST ANOTHER SLEEPY MORNING

It's a sleepy Sunday morning
and I feel someone plop down on the bed.
Through squinting eyes I see a beautiful smile
and hear Anna whisper sweetly, "Hi, Daddy."
I ask her if she had a good sleep
and she nods up and down.
Maureen carries Allan in next in a fresh dry diaper
and he drops in beside Anna
as he shouts happily, "Good morning!"
The clock on my bureau and my plans for the day
both seem to disappear as we play, tickle, laugh,
and hide together under the blankets
until Mommy yells, "Breakfast time!"
Simultaneously, their feet swing towards
the edge of the bed
and with their fists full of sheets,
they slide down to the floor
and bid me, "Bye, bye,"
as they race out the door towards the kitchen.
"But you just got here," I yelled,
but they're already down the hallway.
I pick up my pen and write these words down
knowing that I'll soon forget
but not fully certain why
I felt it was so important
to remember.

FEBRUARY 14TH

Early Valentine's morning
it suddenly dawned on me that I had forgotten
to buy something for my wife.
Awestruck by my own lack of thoughtfulness
I combed through my recent memories
for reasons why I hadn't.

Maybe I was too exhausted
from teaching or from being up with the kids
who were fighting a fever.
It might have been the tiring drive
to my mother-in-law's
ear appointment in Edmonton.
Or maybe it was getting up with Maureen
who was suffering
from the same virus and cough
that I had just recovered from.
None of the excuses changed that fact
that I had no gift to give.

I walked out to the kitchen
and the first thing my wife said to me was,
"Thank you for looking after me last night."
Almost instantly my guilt faded away
and after further reflection
her words left me with
a refreshing realization:
Our Valentine's Day had been about
acts of love and giving after all.
They were just of another kind.

CLOSING OF THE DAY

At the closing of each and every day
I lay in our tub and begin to pray.
Forgive me for all of the sins I've done
help and guide me in the day to come.
But the longest part of my evening prayer
are my thanks for life's blessings everywhere.

TEARS TO LAUGHTER

Helplessness and worry hung over our heads
for four days and nights as we watched
our two-year-old son and daughter grow weaker
as they struggled with high temperatures
and a lack of appetite.
An unrelenting cough attacked in waves
every fifteen minutes,
robbing them of vital rest each night.
The doctors reiterated
there was nothing they could do
since the stubborn virus had to take its course.
So we soothed them, kept them hydrated,
and tried our best to manage their fevers.
Their pale faces and listless bodies haunted
my guilt-laden mind
since it was I who brought
the sickness home from school.
Hopelessness sunk my thoughts
into the murky depths
in search of which of my sick students
was sent to school too soon.
Eventually fatigue and self-pity

broke me down and I cried hidden away
in our master bedroom.
Condensed emotions precipitated
like a cloudburst
before drying my eyes and returning
back to where I was needed.
I will never forget the day
the glorious sun emerged.
The viral siege had lifted
and the fevers were gone.
They began to eat and run
and we began to laugh.
We gave thanks to God for giving us strength
as we watched our young children
suffer for the first time
and for what seemed to us a miracle,
like the dead being brought back
to life again.

TO MY CHILDREN

———

I always want my children to know
that I love them
and since their arrival
they have forever changed
my life for the good
because they bring out the best in me,
teaching me patience,
allowing me to be my true self,
content in the knowledge
that I was now a giver and receiver
of pure unconditional love.

GOODNIGHT KISSES

After a relaxing and lazy Sunday
together as a family
I waited for the kids to fall asleep
when I heard my son Allan ask,
"Can I kiss and hug you, Daddy?"
I got to my feet and went
to receive his nightly gift of love.
I went on to collect
similarly tender gestures from his sisters,
not unlike the goodnight kiss
that I used to deliver to my own mother
when I was a boy,
as I prepared to cast off those
secure maternal ties
before drifting alone into the darkness
towards the inevitable
and unpredictable
land of dreams.

SCHOOL NIGHT

At the end of a long working day
after the kids are fed and bathed
the time comes to prop
my feet up on the ottoman
in front of our flickering gas fireplace
to listen to my seven year old read to me
as our four-year-old twins
play and snuggle under
the tent blanket
that they hastily pitched

over my outstretched legs.
Prayers and storytime shortly follow
as I regale them with tales from books,
memory, or imagination.
As I improvise on the silly actions and voices
of fictional characters,
my playful efforts are repaid to me three-fold
by the sheer delight portrayed on their faces
as they peek in and out from behind the bedspread.
Soon they are tucked into their own beds
after an exchange of hugs from me
and good-night kisses from them on my cheek.
I leave their rooms knowing that every night
won't be like this one
especially when I'm in a rush on a school night
and there's so little time to fit it all in,
but I'll try tomorrow
providing that I'm not too tired or cranky
and the kids aren't overly engaged
in front of a screen.
Or maybe I'll take the time to write
a few lines of poetry like I've done tonight
but I doubt I'll be doing both
since parent and poet are in themselves
full-time occupations.

FLOWER

Julie Radford at age fifty
travelled around the world
from the distant Philippines
to Northern Alberta, Canada
to marry a farmer she got to know
by hand-written letters

and stayed by his side
for six months until he died.
In the following years,
she ran their farm,
tended to the animals,
and showed kindness
to neighbours and seniors.
Her warmth was felt instantaneously
as she smiled and shook hands
with me, a stranger.

In the summer she brought to share
fresh onions and lettuce
grown in her garden
and at Christmas
she dropped off sticky rice
wrapped in banana leaves,
tasting like sweet tea,
before quickly departing
without want of a thank you.

Giving was something Julie did often
no matter what the season,
and one February night,
while trudging across
a wintry pasture,
she gave her life,
as God welcomed her,
the most beautiful flower
to have ever blossomed
on that snowy prairie field.
I now look forward to one day
visiting our friend Julie
in God's peaceful
garden paradise.

CHRISTMAS TREE

My wife and I arrived to a trailer
that was rented by my wife's friends
from the tropical Philippines.
These recent immigrants
had landed in Canada only short months before.
In my own language they welcomed me
the lone Canadian
with open arms and smiles
making me feel very much at home.

My wife Maureen joined those
in the busy kitchen
helping prepare the rice
and a variety of Canadian
and Asian dishes
as I was shown to the living room
where I sunk down into a cozy couch.

I noticed a Christmas tree standing
in a lonely corner of the living room
with green artificial limbs
baring the weight
of countless flickering lights.
As I stared at all the colours
it brought to mind many joyful memories
of Christmases spent together
with my family back home.
The scrumptious food,
the stories, laughter, fun,
and that all important sense
of what it was to belong.

As I looked away
I wiped the sweat from my forehead
and took a sip from the cold drink
that Maureen had placed at my feet.
I never asked why they had left their tree up
for so long until now,
the middle of summer.
I believed that I already knew.

PAC-MAN

With the supper finished
and cold refreshments now in hand
23 men and women
from the distant Philippines
and 4 Canadians
waited impatiently in a crowded living room
for the upcoming pay-per-view boxing match
that would soon be televised live
from Las Vegas, Nevada.
Manny Pacquiao, the Filipino people's champion,
came from nothing, selling cigarettes
on the poor streets of Manila
and was now fighting the Puerto Rican belt holder.

Although I could not understand
what the people around me
were saying to each other
I could hear the excitement and nervousness
in the tone of their voices
as Pacquiao prepared to fight
his larger opponent.
Many of those around me
joined in with proud voices

as their national anthem
was sung in Tagalog.

Soon the room grew quiet.
The men leaned in from the edge of their seats
and the women's faces retreated behind pillows
as the boxing match began.
Every lightning-fast jab delivered by Pacquiao
brought thunderous claps and jubilant cheers.
Every resounding blow taken by Pacquiao
caused the women to shriek and the men to wince
with painful grimaces.
The rounds quickly passed and the excitement grew
as their national hero began to dominate
with his speed and might.

With the fight nearly over
I looked at the intense emotions
that were still playing out
on the faces around me.
It was then that it occurred to me
that it didn't really matter
that some of the people watching
didn't even like boxing
or that none of them
would ever receive a share
of the thirty million dollar prize
if their beloved fighter won.
What mattered most to them and the millions
of their countrymen abroad
was that they sincerely believed
Pacquiao was fighting for them.

SANTA'S HERE!
(TO THE HACKETT FAMILY)

Just days before Christmas, my family and I
were gathered in our home
with my sister-in-law's family
newly arrived from the Philippines.
Only the adults knew
that our neighbour was on his way over
dressed as Santa
to surprise the children with presents.
Unaware, the six kids were seated
on the stairs waiting to have their picture taken
when all of a sudden Santa's face
appeared in the door window.
This six-foot-three, four-hundred-pound
tattooed gentleman in a Santa suit
entered with a jolly, booming voice
wishing all a "Merry Christmas"
and the kids went clear foolish,
running crazily in all directions,
screaming loudly with terror and delight.
Within mere seconds
the youngsters had flocked to the couch
and perched beside the only adult
who was sitting down.
(The rest of us were up holding cameras.)
The three youngest children were squeezed
behind the three oldest,
each staring in shock and disbelief
as Santa sat down and began
calling out their names.

In that moment you could sense
an amazing calm set in

LEN MAC LELLAN

as each child happily sat on his knee
to accept their gift.
Then quick as a wink
he was gone out the door
as they crowded the window
wondering where he was going next.

In the minds of those children
and in my own, Valleyview, Alberta
was for a night transformed
from being your typical
snowbound boreal town
to becoming a most unexpected
land of Christmas wonder
not even a block down
from the North Pole.

LANGUAGE NOT REQUIRED

———

Under a beautiful blue-sapphire sky
I stand smiling
atop the sparkling crown
and watch in amusement
as my son Allan and his cousin Nikko
from the Philippines
toboggan joyfully down
the icy shoulder
towards the glistening silvery ripples
at the foot of the hill.
Quite on purpose they lean over
and crash into fits
of hysterical giggling
and intermingled words
of English and Tagalog.

In this moment of sheer jubilance
it doesn't matter
that neither four year old
knows what the other is saying
because when it comes to having fun
language is really
only optional.

RESTLESSNESS AND DOUBT

WESTWARD

I wonder if my descendants
having grown mature and reflective
will think upon my name
and ponder how I lived my life
as I have reflected on
my pioneering ancestor
Ronald Mac Lellan
who sailed west with his two brothers
across a vast sea of uncertainty.

I too journeyed from the East
across wide, unfamiliar territory
yet the inconveniences I encountered
in the comfort of my Ford Tempo
were minor compared
to the hardships that Ronald endured.

Yet each of us still ventured westward
carrying with us our faith and future hopes,
as well as a lingering sense of doubt
about if we had done
the right thing.

DOUBT AND FAITH

After Maureen turned thirty
and with myself in my forties
I remember wondering

if we would ever be parents.
It was going on five years
since we were married
yet we were still waiting
for the children to come.

With each passing year
we saw newer couples
with newborn sons or daughters
yet I wasn't wholly happy for them
since their happiness was not ours.
Selfishly, I could barely manage a smile
when I was around them.

During those moments
of frustration and doubt,
I would think about a story
my late Aunt Irene told me
about my grandfather,
Alec Dan Mac Lellan,
who married at age forty-eight
and had twelve children
with my grandmother Marie.
One day a curious neighbour
who was passing by
asked my grandfather
about how someone as old as he was
could afford to look after so many children.
My grandfather, in all his faith and wisdom,
quoted a bible passage that I've since repeated
whenever I felt that my faith
was being tested.
He simply said,
"God will provide."
For me, that says it all.

SHIP TO SHORE

I am on a ship at sea.
Where and why are uncertain.
I get the sense it is military,
steel grey, like the ocean and sky
below and above me.
I see no guns.
I feel excitement as I ready my uniform
for the parade on deck.
Beyond there is land somewhere out of reach.
It is the good pay that keeps me anchored here.

The phone rings and I jump
to ready attention from my restless slumber.
It is early and still dark.
It is my father wondering
if I received the twins' birthday cards.
Crankily I remind him that we're three hours behind
and it's not yet 6 a.m.
Dad apologizes and tells me
that he will call back later.

Now I can't get back to sleep
because I just remembered
that this will be the first day
back with my students since before Easter.
With nothing to do but wait
I try to decipher my dream's meaning
and can't help but draw similarities
between it and the dreams I've had before.
Sometimes I'm a pilot readying my fighter plane
before I take off into battle.
Sometimes I am an infantryman
huddled among other soldiers whose faces I know,

waiting in fear for the command to charge.
In each case I'm always far from home
doing my duty as best I can
but never being allowed to leave, waiting nights,
years, decades, for my service to be over.

Sadly, the war never seems to end
and inner restfulness is never fully found
yet a semblance of peace remains
like a spark of hope that one day our toil here
on the Western Front will be done
and I will wake one morning
to find myself home again.

ALONE

"Can you play a few tunes, Wib?"
I asked, as I glanced down at his dusty guitar case
leaning in the corner of his small apartment.
Wib shook his head, exhaled the last draw
of smoke from his lungs and said,
"I haven't played for months,
since I had my last drink."
Sensing my disappointment
at not being able to listen to him play
he clarified his position
by recounting for me in detail stories
from his past musical performances.
He pointed out that during those times
a pattern had been playing out for him
but he never took notice until recently.
Things were now as clear
as an empty glass.

Where Wib once enjoyed
playing the music and sipping beer,
crowded by shaky tables and spilled ashtrays,
now the guitar was but a reminder.
When all was said and sung,
with tomorrow promising
a headache and sore fingertips,
there could be no happiness,
but only a deep sense of loneliness felt,
at the thought of sleeping on an empty couch
or the weariness
of staggering home alone.

MASTER PLANNER

I think of it as being a friend to myself
when I open my closet door
and see my clothes for the day
pressed and neatly hanging
or when I turn the page
of my teaching plan book
and find the day's activities
organized and ready to go.
It always feels comforting
when today's preparations make
my life tomorrow a little bit easier.

I often get the same reassuring feelings
when I appreciate how
important events in my life
have come together
as if by pre-plan or design.
Events that led me down
the road of teaching for example,

or led me to my wife's side,
or just how I sometimes land
at the right place at the right time,
make me a believer
in coincidences or luck no longer.
I truly feel that there is
a master plan at work in all our lives
and I try to fulfill it with blind faith
keeping watch for the
inspirational sign posts
that continually guide me
along the way.

I pray for God, the master planner,
to be with me and my family
on our spiritual journey
as we learn and grow
for your greater purpose,
knowing that each day passed
brings us closer to you.

THE LUNCH BOX

———

During the summer of 1990
I needed to travel back and forth to work
along a scenic thirty-three kilometre
stretch of highway that skirted
the rugged Cape Breton coastline.
My parents let it be known
that they couldn't spare the family car
and that I would likely have to hitchhike.
Undaunted and in need of tuition money
I felt I had no choice but to expose myself
to all the uncertainties of thumbing for rides.

My grandfather wisely advised me to carry
my father's aluminum lunch box to work,
saying that if drivers saw it
they would think I was heading to a job
or travelling back home after a tiring workday.
He was right, since a drive
was always found in the morning
that brought me to work on time.

Hitching rides on meandering Route 19
in the evening after work
was a more daunting task
since the steady midday stream of traffic
had dwindled to little more than a trickle.
What got me through those moonlight marches
were the keen-eyed motorists
who kindly pulled over with the offer of a lift
after spotting the glint from my father's lunch can.

Years later I still wonder if some part of me
is still out there on that lonely stretch of road
having dreamt of it on many occasions.
The dreams vary little
with me treading under a starless sky,
with blurred Atlantic waves
crashing on the rocky shore to my left
and the shadowy wooded highlands
rising on my right.
Ahead through the gloom
I see the road curve
before being swallowed
into unapproachable darkness.
Having been here before and not wanting
to let fear take the upper hand
I merely hold up my father's lunch can

and right on cue
headlights will appear.

EBAY FORAY

After the excitement
of the auction win dies down
buyer's remorse creeps in
after realizing I've spent too much
at a time when I should be saving
yet aware I may soon be back chasing
those elusive best deals
that will make me feel like a winner
if only for a few moments.

MIND GAMES

He couldn't get her out of his head.
Whenever he spotted her
he stole adoring glances.
When he was alone he filled
his quiet mind with thoughts
of her brown eyes and red lips.
Although they had never been
more than casual friends
he felt that he knew her intimately
having spent many hours alone
walking, laughing, and holding her
deep in the wishing well of his imagination.
He nurtured many of the hopeful possibilities
until his infatuation fabricated

what felt like real emotions.
He kept this secret to himself.

Concerning another, he couldn't
seem to quiet his quarrelsome mind.
At seeing her at a distance his heart dropped.
He filled empty hours with dark
intolerable thoughts of her.
Although they knew not each other well
he was convinced they were enemies.
He imagined her snubs,
insults, and negative exchanges
as if he was preparing for the conflict to come.
In the hours between their meetings
he almost took pleasure
in contemplating her suffering.
He said nothing and his
unhappiness smoldered.

He wondered how he got like this.
How his good and passionate mind
could mislead his own heart.
It could be a persistent betrayer of sorts
convincing himself to believe
that things are different
than they actually are in truth.
It conjures emotions that are best left unstirred
while his spirit suffers
the disappointment and frustration
at not being able to express them.
He is terrified of the shame that would be his
if he only could.

STUCK IN NEUTRAL

These past summer days of rainfall and sunshine
are very reflective of the coolness and warmth
felt in the presence of four young couples we know.
Two of the married couples broke apart
while the other two pairs were joined together.
The combination of the resulting
negative and positive energies
has left me emotionally numb,
feeling neither sad nor happy.
Recognizing that my wife and I
were in the middle of things,
we have tried to help them all.
Eventually a feeling of gladness
and gratefulness came over me
at not having to stand in any of their shoes,
at journey's bitter end
nor its sweet beginning.

DREAM

Last night I had a dream that I didn't share
with my wife in the morning
because in it I saw a young woman I once knew
as she took me places where we once visited
during my university days in beautiful Northern Maine
so many springs ago.

She was as I remembered, energetic and adventurous,
laughing nervously as we climbed down slippery stones
beside roaring river rapids or sat on the gentle hillside,
eating cold ham sandwiches and drinking warm lemonade

that I had carried up in my backpack.
With painful honesty and genuine openness
we spoke of the future roads
we were likely to follow after the summer,
knowing full well mine
would lead me far from hers.

Accepting that her life was there
and my career was still uncertain
we parted as true friends
as I left for Cape Breton,
knowing that I'd never be back,
with little consolation except
we would always have letters.
We seldom kept in touch
as our lives went on and in quick succession
I found a teaching job,
a new place to live,
and little time left to reminisce
about how she was doing
or if she missed me
after those wonderful days
we had shared in the springtime.

Several years passed and I was excited to receive
a letter from her with some good news.
She was now happily married
with a husband and two children
and enclosed was their picture.
A beautiful family.
I smiled, not helping but to notice
that her husband looked just like me.

PEACE OF MIND

It was four in the morning
and I could not sleep.
Stress and my overly busy mind
had once again interrupted
what I had hoped would be a good night's rest.
In the quiet darkness I made my way
to our living room window
and searched the distant flickering lights
as I silently prayed to God
for some calm and reassurance.
Early the next morning I awoke in bed
to the sounds of giggling
and found our three playful children
jostling under our covers.
I don't know how long we played and laughed
but in those light-hearted minutes
I became wonderfully aware
that the peace and contentment
that I had lost sight of
was really never far from our sides.

DISTRACTED DRIVING

Distraction can easily lead to harm
if not kill you altogether.
I have seen drivers talking on phones,
applying makeup, reading books,
and even fornicating behind the wheel.
I could hardly keep my eyes on the road.
How many more accidents will have to occur
before motorists are no longer

driven to distraction?
Maybe you are one of those dreaded multitaskers
who finds driving a bore, and pulls out
something interesting to leaf through
such as this poetry book
skimming through with ease,
scanning line by line
with little or no perception
of the hairpin curve dead ahead.

LENTEN JOURNEY

Glimpses of brilliant morning sunlight
filtered through bare branches
of the poplar trees clustered near our home.
It was as if nature itself had held its cool breath
as I too paused to observe a moment of silence
in wonderment of the beautiful winter day that was.

Not wishing to waste precious moments of fresh dawn air
I ventured out and felt my senses awaken
after too many sleepy hours indoors.
With no biting winds to hurry my steps forward
I settled into a relaxed pace
as I focused on the rhythmic crunching
of my mukluks upon untrampled snow.
Along the wayside lost strands of summer wheat
stood defiantly above the snow.
Each head and stalk was adorned with
sparkling ice crystals that were formed
in the darkness before sunrise.
All appeared motionless in this frozen world
except for my long shadow that glided atop the road,
shading the streaks of dirty brown ice upon it.

LEN MAC LELLAN

Eventually I reached the church entrance
and I quietly entered in time for confession.
After my burdens of conscience had been lifted
I journeyed home, breathing deeply and joyfully,
feeling lighter and more at peace,
like a soul made new
once again.

CLOSE ENCOUNTER

My wife watched from the bleachers
as I warmed up doing stretches
on the soft green grass behind home plate
when we heard a loud booming voice
echo from the parking lot.
Reaching for my toes
I glanced sideways and saw
a large woman approaching us.
Shielding my eyes from the sun
I observed that she was not
a handsome woman
with rounded masculine facial features.
The lady sat down beside my wife
while bellowing insults at the male companions
who had accompanied her.
The young men walked away
and the woman settled down.
Seemingly out of left field
the woman asked Maureen,
"So does your ole man beat ya?"
I froze, as if time itself ceased moving forward,
not knowing exactly what to do or say.
Without hesitation the woman added,
"Mine beats me most of the time."

Maureen reassured her saying,
"My husband's not like that,"
and I watched the woman's countenance
soften into an expression of genuine surprise.
Her associates soon returned
with news that they were playing
at the lower diamond.
As the group of them walked quietly away
I thanked my stars that we didn't
have to face them in the innings to come
watching our softballs
blast off their bats like rockets
knowing that there was little hope
of recovering them
as we had no ladder
to reach the moon.

TO FORGIVE IS DIVINE

Have you ever been betrayed
or unfairly judged by someone
whom you'd shown only kindness and friendship
and then accepted an apology
because it was the right thing to do,
although deep down in your heart
you still had not yet forgiven them?
In such situations an eye for an eye
doesn't seem that unreasonable
when the wounds are fresh
and one cannot understand
the reason for it all.

I cannot be healed on my own
so I wait with my self-pity as counsel,

praying for the light to scatter my darkness,
for happiness to overcome my pain,
and for truth and peace
to conquer the anger I now nurture.
I call out to the Lord because I know
He will hear my voice,
and I can only hope
that He will save me
from myself.

THE SNUB

Words used as weapons
can cut fast and deep to our core
but what of silence?
I do not mean in terms
of peace and quiet, but rather
the dark punishing kind.

The silent snub is a sinister
and resentful type of sword
that is wielded most effectively
by a non-confrontational
and unhappy person
who is not yet ready
to communicate or to forgive.
Most of the time you don't feel
the snub's blade pressing against you
until you are in proximity of
its angry and vindictive presence.

Trying to break the silence too early
or attempting to restore the peace
by pretending that the snub does not exist

often intensifies the snubber's efforts
consequently upsetting the mind
and piercing the heart of the powerless victim.
Time seems to drag on
while the snubber holds something against you.
Eventually it gets under your skin
to the point that you become
as wounded and unhappy as the perpetrator
and you begin to take your frustrations
out on those oblivious to the situation.
The only remedy is avoidance
and not being in range of the subtle
and purposeful mistreatments
that lie in wait.
Hence the internal injuries
will be minimized.

Fighting fire with fire
sounds like a sound solution
but it takes huge amounts of energy
and it could draw out a brief cold war
into a perpetual ice age.
It may harmlessly begin
with one-upmanship
those momentary gratifications
and fleeting victories over the other.
The longer it goes the greater the danger
that the mind games will degrade
into mutual feelings akin to hatred
all the while stubbornly pretending
that you're happy around each other
when you're not.
This malicious manoeuvring never fails
to fill me with guilt and unhappiness
knowing that such negativity
poisons my soul

LEN MAC LELLAN

while knowing full well that I can
be a better man than this.

MY TWO CENTS' WORTH

I used to barter new money for old,
such as unearthed denarii
hidden by long dead Roman soldiers
or the lost silver ecus sea salvaged
from eighteenth-century wrecks
or well-worn copper tokens
that once lined the pockets
of provincial pioneers.
Coins that once passed
from hand to hand long ago
and were spent on now forgotten things
will circulate no more.
I knew that each coin
would eventually outlast me
and that one day I would
leave them all behind.
It wasn't too difficult to let them go.
After all, it was only money.

EVOLUTION OF A COLLECTOR

As a boy I spent many after-school hours
in peaceful solitude
stretched out on my bed
pouring over my coin collection
imagining the origins and stories
of each copper or silver piece

that was carefully clasped
between my fingers.

Later on, the coins failed to glitter
and sparkle as they once had
in those earlier years.
I stopped showing them to anyone anymore
and couldn't find the time
to sit and enjoy my hobby,
when all I felt was tired
after work or playtime
with our children.

My wife had no interest
in numismatics
and did not approve
of me needlessly spending
money on my collection
when it could be better utilized
for groceries and other necessities.

It had turned out to be a rather lonely hobby
guarding something that no longer
added to my self-worth.
Eventually I found someone who was willing
to take them off my hands for the right price.
I was very happy for them when they did.
But I did not envy them.

GOD'S MERCIFUL RAIN

I sit facing our living room window
with my eyes closed
listening to that almost

long-forgotten song
that the rain makes
as it taps out its random
soothing drum roll.

Through the top of the window
I stare at a herd
of grey nimbus clouds
racing by in unison
as if driven by the whip
of a wild Western wind.
Lowering my gaze
I watch the relentless gusts
torment the neighbour's trees
as their limbs violently
flail and strike at unseen foes
in every direction.

Where insistent arid winds
hastened past us a day before
now drops of mercy descend
bringing relief to the farmers
and a glorious resurrection
to a mummified earth.

An inferno rages in Fort McMurray,
akin to an out-of-control furnace,
untameable, unquenchable,
devouring all in its path.
What if the smoky winds
were to drive it in our direction?
I choose not to imagine
the swath of fiery devastation
that would consume
our parched poplar groves
and our houses of sticks

for there would be nothing
for us to do but run.

I push out the hellish thoughts
and stare again out the glass
that separates my family
from drenching sheets of rain
that wrap around our home
like wet security blankets.

Closing my eyes
for a few moments
I am lulled and comforted
by the rain's life-saving beat.
I almost dread
to hear it end.

FAITH AND HOPE

Waiting is an inevitable reality
but I need not think of it
as a lesson in anything
or worse as a punishment
from a higher power.

I now understand that waiting
is but a slight hesitation
while all is made ready
before certain events unfold
in God's plan for us.

At the right moment
our wishes will come to be
according to His higher plan

LEN MAC LELLAN

conceived better than my
imperfect mind ever could.

The frustration of waiting
for my sister-in-law's visa
or the coming of our second child
still overshadows me, however,
there is much I cannot see.

I believe that this wait time
is undoubtedly necessary
for everyone's best interests
and I need not understand it
nor question why.

I must patiently trust
that my most worthy and just
heartfelt prayers will be granted
with each passing day
bringing them closer to fruition.

CHRISTMAS MORN

———

In the soft glow of this early morning
the storm of excitement has finally subsided.
Many of the brightly wrapped mysteries
have been hurriedly solved
and each child now sits
like the proud keeper of personal plunder
piled into the profile of a crooked lighthouse.
With a lookout's eye
some dive from coastline cushions
into the wrinkled waves of sparkling paper

vigilantly searching for their name
on any remaining pieces of sunken treasure.

Soon there is nothing left for me to do
but haul in the discarded
paper and plastic from the floor
and unceremoniously stuff it
by the handful into garbage bags
to be later hauled away and buried.
This is not so unusual
as I've often utilized a similar technique
whenever I've needed to depose of
unwelcome emotions that begin to sink in
when I am reminded of those
who couldn't be with us
on Christmas morn.

I try to look on the bright side
and focus instead on
the children's smiling faces
and I smile too
as I stare eastward through our window
at the newborn sun
and look forward to all the good things
that will likely follow with its rising.

REVOLUTION

My body is in revolt and has laid siege
with two and a half months
of cramps, diarrhea, blood,
flatulence, and fatigue.
I starve myself of once familiar
food and drinks,

while clamouring for meagre
gluten-free rations.
I must kill the carbohydrates
that threaten to drag on
this internal civil war.

Disheartened and under duress
I desperately plan out
healthy measures
in hopes of a peaceful armistice,
or maybe my soul could reach out
to my physical side
to discuss the terms of my surrender,
if only I was convinced
he was listening.

FELLOW TRAVELLERS

Old friend, you took me as far as you could go
when you walked me through those unfamiliar
and solitary paths after my arrival here in the West.
You befriended me and helped alleviate
my underlying fears and frustrations
simply by listening and empathizing
through similar stories of your own.
After a visit with you I felt lighter
and less alone in the world,
having had my anxieties justified
and my inner peace restored
for the moment.
I thank you for that.

I never saw you much after I got married
and then never at all after you died

except maybe in a dream.
How good it would be
to have a visit with you again.
You who once was a healer at heart
and now me, years later,
a most irritable and anxious patient.
Lonely but not alone,
I could meet you maybe somewhere
in the middle of here and there,
like fellow travelers happy for company,
with no expectations
of the remedy for my ailment,
but just looking once again
for the understanding
of my suffering
in your eyes.

GIVE YOURSELF TIME

If you're always in a hurry, give yourself time.
If life has become a worry, give yourself time.
Nerves begin to wear, running here and there,
with no room to spare, give yourself time.

If you're travelling on the road, give yourself time.
When you tire of heavy loads, give yourself time.
To be at your best, save yourself the stress,
park it for a rest, give yourself time.

If you are running with the kids, give yourself time.
If you're ready to blow your lid, give yourself time.
You will only lose, lighting a short fuse,
it's for us to choose, give yourself time.

LEN MAC LELLAN

If working is a thankless chore, give yourself time.
If you always rush out the door, give yourself time.
For your own health's sake, take a little break,
it's only minutes late, give yourself time.

If you've married a loving wife, give yourself time.
She can extend your happy life, give yourself time.
For the best effect, do not waste a sec,
try to reconnect, give yourself time.

If you miss those moments alone, give yourself time.
Put away the busy cell phone, give yourself time.
Enjoy books again, or creative pen,
reach your inner friend, give yourself time.

GRATITUDE

In solitude I lay
with some semblance of calm
waiting to be wheeled into day surgery
when all of a sudden
my doubts and fears
like unwanted guests
walked into my mind
and pulled up a pillow beside me.

Anxiety makes such a cold
and unwelcome bedfellow
so I kicked it out and focused my mind
on thanking God instead.
Like a joyful mantra
I began repeating in my mind
over and over again,

"Thank you, God. Thank you,
God. Thank you, God..."

Admittedly, I did not know at first
what I was thanking Him for,
but the words themselves
had an immediate
soothing effect on me.
My heavy heartedness was lightened
and my attitude became cheerful
as I continued to repeat,
"Thank you, God. Thank you,
God. Thank you, God…"

The simple words and thoughts of gratitude
seemed to pour out from a part of me
that rarely spoke
except in my deepest prayers.
I began to visualize my life
from the present moment
back to my childhood
picturing the faces of all the people
who were good to me
and I thanked God
for putting all of them
in my life.

I have been reassured that God
has been with me
from the beginning until now
and He would get me through this
as He always has done
and with that I found myself
floating upon an inner river of peace

that I wished would never end
lying on a hospital gurney
all encompassed in the warmth
of love and gratitude.

THROUGH A TEACHER'S EYES

AUGUSTA PARKER

I was able to care about
and teach my students
only because you
as a principal and a friend
cared about
and reached me first.

AUGUST GALES

Paper piles rise up on my desk
like white caps on the heavy seas.
Late August gales are whispering
and my mind isn't yet at ease.

Opening day is our due heading
students gather on yonder shore.
Little worries weigh like anchors
slowing my progress, aft and fore.

Fear not, this storm will surely pass
if we ride it out together.
God will bring peace amid our lives
no matter what kind of weather.

Should the barometer fall fast
say a prayer without delay.
Follow God's light of hope and love
and you'll make it through okay.

I thank God for bringing us here
and for our friends who help so much.

Those who make these days seem easy
during weather changes and such.

Let us rest our hands from our wheels
let our sails slip from their masts.
Simple faith has calmly floated
our boats to safe harbour, at last.

ENCOURAGEMENT

Most young children will remember
long after they have aged and grown
the words like seeds you have planted
of kindness or unkindness sown.
Feed and weed them with love and truth
and your efforts won't fail to yield.
Reveal the pride you feel inside
as they grow stronger in their field.

HOW WE COMMUNICATE

Out of the blue
as I sat at the staff-room table
quietly reading the newspaper
a younger staff member
three chairs down from mine
asked me if I owned a cell phone.
I answered, "No."
Without hesitation she blurted,
"That's weird."
In the moments that followed
I couldn't help but think how unkind it was

for someone to voice that it was weird
just because I didn't own a cell phone.
Secretly, I think I would rather be judged
as being weird
than to be considered
unkind.

OUT OF THE ORDINARY

"Grade 5 sucks!" I heard
as one of my several
behaviourally challenged students
shouted at me as he made his way again
to the principal's office.
There will be others to follow
in this our first week in September.

This is the smallest class that I've ever taught
yet it contains the most
behavioural needs I ever had.
I can't recall my mind and body
feeling this tired all at the same time.

But I know it will be a good year
because they will have
a safe and consistent classroom environment
that will nurture success and acceptance
within our classroom family.

My biggest concern is if I get too good
at reaching the minds and hearts
of the most challenging students
I may be seen as some kind
of behavioural specialist

LEN MAC LELLAN

and I'll never be given
the opportunity to teach
a regular class again.

EULOGY FOR A YOUNG STUDENT

For me, your grade 5 teacher,
this will be my final progress report for you.
I just wanted to let you know
how well you've done in this life.

I am sorry that I can't recall
if you met your IPP goals in math,
or even what reading level you reached.
However, one thing I am sure of is that
the master teacher, Jesus,
must be so very proud of you.
You worked hard and long
on the important subjects
of love, compassion, and forgiveness.
Your loving smile glowed for everyone,
friends and foe alike,
your compassion was for all,
and you always forgave
those who offended you.

When it was you who made the mistakes
by raising your voice
or your hand against another
you always reconciled by saying sorry
and by giving a hug.

All was forgiven.
I'm sure Jesus will say to you

you have learned your lessons well
and because of the excellence you've shown
in these essential areas
on behalf of all who knew you
you are hereby promoted to the next level.
You have passed with flying colours.

HE WILL GIVE YOU STRENGTH

―――――

As an experienced teacher used to being in control
nothing makes me feel more alone or afraid
than on those rare alarming occasions
when I have felt the impact
of slamming doors, flying objects,
kicks, or punches.
I must admit to myself
that in those darkest and fiercest of moments,
when I was pushed to my emotional limits,
I was tempted to hurt the student back
with a vengeance.
Thankfully I never fought back
choosing instead to withdraw to where
I could find support and a place of calm
where I could breathe normally again.

I may never know the true extent
of the anger and suffering
in the life of a student who would choose
to lash out violently.
If I did, I would hope that my understanding
and compassion would eventually smother
the flames of my worst wrath
and resentment against them.
But it often takes time.

LEN MAC LELLAN

Reconciliation with someone who hurt you
does not come easy,
but it starts by taking that time for myself,
talking about it with those who are willing to listen
and by praying to God for healing and forgiveness.
When the time comes to return to teaching again
do not be afraid.
God has chosen us to do His important
and sacred work.
He will give you strength.

CAN I WALK WITH YOU, DADDY?

It was recess time out on the playground
when Alexis threw her arms around my waist,
took my hand in hers and sweetly asked,
"Can I walk with you, Daddy?"

With my brain in teacher mode
I sent her away reminding her
that she should be playing with her friends
since I was on duty and she would only
distract me from watching the other children.
She walked away, turned and waved
with that beautiful smile
before she scaled up the blue monkey bars.

In silent introspection I walked across
the snowy playground wondering how many more
precious offers like that one would I receive in my life
before she stopped asking.
My heart supposed as long as I was a teacher
I would have busy playgrounds to watch over

but I would not always have a
five-year-old daughter.

With that certainty clearly in mind
rarely do I pass up an opportunity to walk with her
knowing that years from now she'll be different
and I'll be retired and longing for
those simple pleasures I once knew
walking hand in hand
with my little girl.

CATCH OUR SPIRIT

"Catch our Spirit"
was a fitting theme for our old school
since many of those who
walked through our doors
had almost instantaneously felt
the warm and welcoming spirit
of our surroundings.
I think that it was the reason why
some students wished to remain so long.

For example, a former student of mine
who could have moved on years ago
could be found standing in the hallway
waving to those who took notice
of her long golden hair
and the beautiful colours of radiant light
surrounding her body
giving her the semblance
of an angel.
She liked it there.

NECK TIE

It is extraordinary
the things children will do
for those they love.
The lengths some would go to
not have their parents fight.

Such as stealing
my neck tie just so
there was something to take home
to later surprise Dad with
in those pivotal moments
before he beat her mom.
Given as an unexpected gift of sorts
that might avert or distract
from the impending violence
if only for a while.

If a person didn't know
all the circumstances
one might judge the unlawful youth
as being misguided
or lacking moral principles,
as I once judged,
before I understood
that a child would go
to astonishing lengths
in order to deter the hateful words
and brutality between
the two people she loved most.

TRAP LINE

While waiting for
an education conference to begin
I began a short conversation
with a lady sitting across the table.
She was teaching at a school to the south
and from her white hair and warm tone
I assumed that she was not new to the profession.
Our schools, it turned out, were similar in size,
each meeting the needs of Aboriginal students,
many of whom were Cree or of Métis heritage.
We shared our stories about similar frustrations
over student absenteeism and that by high school
many of our promising Indigenous students
had dropped out.

As the main conference speaker
readied to climb the stairs to take centre stage
my new teacher friend reminded me
that educators can only do so much
to encourage students to do
what we think will bring them happiness.
There are often circumstances
in their lives that are beyond our control.
She concluded our conversation
with a brief story.

At her school the year before
after much hard work
a bright Aboriginal girl graduated with honours
to the delight of her teachers.
Wanting her to succeed further
they helped her apply to Edmonton
where she was accepted at the university

and accommodations were arranged
not far from where she would attend classes.

The girl didn't stay for more than a couple of days
before she quit and went home.
For in her mind there was little room
for books, lectures,
and the expectations of others,
when all she really wanted to do
was to get back home
to her grandfather's trap line.

LOSING CONNECTIONS

I sat down among coworkers
who stared down at wireless devices
and seemed quite oblivious to my presence
outside their cyber world.
It is a lonely place amidst such company
and I was tempted to reveal my presence
by boldly reaching out to the "texter" nearest to me
with a kind word or the gentlest touch
if only to simply say, "I'm here."

I chose instead to sit in subdued silence
envisioning similar types of dilemmas
that may have occurred
with the emergence of past technologies.

Perhaps Thomas Watson
used to get annoyed
standing beside Alexander Graham Bell
thinking the great inventor

was taking much too long
on the telephone.

Or possibly how impatient
Captain Smith may have felt
as he helplessly waited
for his wireless operator
to dash out the final SOS
as the unsinkable liner
went down.

BRAVE FACE

Day after day, year after year
amidst personal turmoil,
relationship dysfunctions and insecurities,
our school staff still puts on a brave face
when given opportunities to bestow
priceless gifts to countless needy children.
Gifts that may be strangely absent
even within ourselves,
such as a sense of belonging,
a love for oneself,
and an unwavering hope for the future.
Educators may indeed be broken
but by God's mercy and His holy intercessions,
these most imperfect servants,
through their faithful service,
surely become truly blessed.

CO-WORKERS WITH CHRIST

Our school staff is a caring family
brought together by God
to teach and to perform
good works for others.
Our judgmental natures
and our petty sibling rivalries
sometimes divide us
but we still come together
with the shared purpose
of enriching the lives
of our students every day.

Since the tragic passing of our librarian
I have honestly felt the work
of the Holy Spirit among my colleagues
as we all have become a little more patient
and a lot more forgiving of each other.
Maybe it was her parting gift to us
that through her loss
we would gain a new appreciation
of how limited our time together really is.
It's a sobering reminder
that we can always do
a better job of taking care
of our brothers and sisters
in the precious time
that we have remaining.

THE GIFT

During bus supervision at the high school
I heard someone call my name.
I turned and saw two Cree students
walking towards me.
"You used to be my teacher,"
one of them said.
"Do you remember me?"
Not knowing who he was, I told him I did,
but he quickly put me to the test
and asked, "What's my name?"
Having no idea,
I looked carefully at his face
and saw something familiar about his eyes
and his name came to mind.
I said his name and his head
jolted back in surprise.
He smiled and appeared pleased
that I actually remembered him.

Proudly he told me he was in grade 12
and that he remembered
when I was his grade 5 teacher
and how I told his class how strict I was
because I had been in the army.
"And you were strict,"
he continued,
"but it helped me to be good
so I could learn stuff.
Not like those nice teachers."

I laughed as we walked on
and he put his arm around my shoulder
and squeezed me in saying,

LEN MAC LELLAN

"I love you, Mr. Mac Lellan."
Before I stepped onto the school bus
I thanked him for giving me
the rare and memorable gift
of appreciation.

As I rode away I carried deep within me
true heartfelt joy
knowing I had once made
such a positive difference
in the life of someone who
I had almost forgotten.

NEW HORIZONS

We reach many horizons in life.
Recently I have reached two
for which I will be forever thankful.
I recently began treatments
for Crohn's disease
and I completed my first book.
I pray that the next horizon reached
will be to help pay for
St. Rita's Gathering Centre.
Beyond that, I look forward to writing
about the inner landscapes
my family and I,
my staff, and my students
will traverse in the future,
knowing that God will be guiding
and providing along the way,
and that with every step
we need not
feel afraid.

If you would like to make a donation
to St. Rita's building fund,
please contact us by phone at 780-524-3425
or by e-mail at stritavalleyview@gmail.com

ABOUT THE AUTHOR

Len Mac Lellan is a husband to Maureen and a father, teacher, storyteller, and poet. Raised in Judique, Cape Breton, Nova Scotia and now raising his own children in Valleyview, Alberta, Mac Lellan has a strong sense of place and community. He takes great joy in his twenty-four years of teaching elementary students at St. Stephen's Catholic School, which is reflected in his being nominated for the 2006 Excellence in Teaching Award and receiving the Excellence in Catholic Education Award in 2012.

When not singing in the church choir or regaling his children – Alexis, Allan, and Anna – with his own stories, he is busy collecting natural and oral history so he can preserve the stories of others. To help keep himself grounded, he notes: "My grandfather, in all his faith and wisdom, quoted a bible passage that I've since repeated whenever I felt that my faith was being tested. He simply said, 'God will provide.'"

Proceeds from the sale of this book will be used to help pay for
St. Rita's Gathering Centre in Valleyview, Alberta.